Ninja CREAMi Cookbook For Beginners

Ninja CREAMi Cookbook For Beginners

365-Day Simple and Easy Recipes from Classic Ice Cream Flavors to Boozy Slushies | Let You Live Healthier and Happier

Sreami Celsen

© Copyright 2021 Sreami Celsen - All Rights Reserved.

In no way is it legal to reproduce, duplicate, or transmit any part of this document by either electronic means or in printed format. Recording of this publication is strictly prohibited, and any storage of this material is not allowed unless with written permission from the publisher. All rights reserved.

The information provided herein is stated to be truthful and consistent, in that any liability, regarding inattention or otherwise, by any usage or abuse of any policies, processes, or directions contained within is the solitary and complete responsibility of the recipient reader. Under no circumstances will any legal liability or blame be held against the publisher for any reparation, damages, or monetary loss due to the information herein, either directly or indirectly.

Respective authors own all copyrights not held by the publisher.

Legal Notice:

This book is copyright protected. This is only for personal use. You cannot amend, distribute, sell, use, quote or paraphrase any part of the content within this book without the consent of the author or copyright owner. Legal action will be pursued if this is breached.

Disclaimer Notice:

Please note the information contained within this document is for educational and entertainment purposes only. Every attempt has been made to provide accurate, up-to-date and reliable, complete information. No warranties of any kind are expressed or implied. Readers acknowledge that the author is not engaging in the rendering of legal, financial, medical or professional advice.

By reading this document, the reader agrees that under no circumstances are we responsible for any losses, direct or indirect, which are incurred as a result of the use of information contained within this document, including, but not limited to, errors, omissions, or inaccuracies.

CONTENT

INTRODUCTION 006

ONE OVERVIEW 007

ICE CREAM 017

MILKSHAKE 053

SORBET 074

SMOOTHIE BOWL 085

CONCLUSION 101

APPENDIX RECIPE INDEX 102

INTRODUCTION

The Ninja CREAMi treat maker is one of the revolutionary advanced ice cream maker machines used to make flavourful ice cream treats at home. It comes with a dual motor base and takes 800Watts power to churn your favourite frozen treat into the cream. It also allows you to add your favourite Mix-in into your favourite ice cream. It is one of the multifunctional kitchen appliances not only make ice cream but is also used to make your favorite milkshake, smoothies, sorbet, gelato, and more. It is easily fitted on your kitchen top like a coffee maker without taking too much space. It comes with 3 CREAMi pits to store and process your frozen treats. Using Ninja CREAMi treat maker you can easily customize your favorite flavor and texture to your ice cream. It also allows you to control your ingredients as per your health conditions. You can make sugary as well as sugar-free healthy treats by using Ninja CREAMi. You can make an experiment with your ice cream by adding different flavors and Mix-in into the cream base.

This cookbook contains 80 delicious and healthy Ninja CREAMi treat recipes. All the recipes written in this cookbook are unique and written in an easy to understandable format. The recipes written in this cookbook are beginning with their exact preparation and processing time followed by a set of step-by-step process instructions. All the recipe ends with its nutritional value information. The nutritional value information will help to keep track of daily calorie consumption. There are few books available in the market on this topic, thanks for choosing my cookbook. I hope you love and enjoy all the Ninja CREAMi treat recipes written in this cookbook.

ONE OVERVIEW

What is Ninja CREAMi?

The Ninja CREAMi is one of the advanced next-generation ice cream churning machines. The machine allows you to make customize treats like ice cream, sorbet, milkshakes, smoothies, and more. You can also customize your favourite flavor by adding your favourite mix-in like chocolates, candies, fruits, and nuts. Using Ninja CREAMi you can make dairy-free, keto-friendly, and gluten-free healthy treats suitable to your taste and moods.

The Ninja CREAMi treat maker works on 800-watt power and comes with a dual motor base main unit that turns your frozen ingredients into the cream. The package includes three pints and lids, one Creamerizer paddle with an outer bowl and lid. The Ninja CREAMi is simple to use, it comes with seven one-touch preset programs like ice cream, sorbet, lite ice cream, smoothie bowl, milkshake, and mix-in. The CREAMi treat maker works on a creamify technology in which the Creamerizer paddle is equipped with a dual drive motor and applies downward pressure to churns frozen treat into the creamiest treat.

How Ninja CREAMi Works?

The Ninja CREAMi is easy to operate and doesn't need setup. The machine is ideal for making ice cream and gelato. You can also make your favourite milkshake and smoothies by using Ninja CREAMi treat maker. To make perfect delicious ice cream you need to create an ice cream base and pour it into a pint container. Place the base-filled pint container into the freezer for at least 24 hours to set. Then place the frozen base container in the Ninja CREAMi treat maker. Choose the appropriate preset function among 7 presets programs. The Ninja CREAMi mixes the base pint container base together within few minutes. It converts your frozen solid base into a creamy mixture. Then add your favorite mix-in like fruit, chocolate, nuts, candies into a container and select the Mix-ins function. The Ninja CREAMi treat maker slowly mixes all the mix-ins equally in the mixture without changing the texture and size of your mix-in.

Quick Start Guide

1. **Plug-in unit:** Plug-in unit into a power socket (If you install outer bowel before the unit is plug-in then the unit will not run).

2. **Install CREAMi pint:** Remove pint lid to check the ingredient base is not frozen at an angle. Place the frozen base pin into the outer bowl.

3. **Install Creamerizer paddle:** Press and hold the paddle latch present on the top side of the outer bowl lid and insert the paddle at the bottom of the lid. To secure the paddle release patch.

4. **Install lid:** Tab of the lid position slightly to the right side of the outer bowl handle till the lines of the handle and lid align. Then rotate the lid clockwise direction to lock.

5. **Install outer bowl:** First Plug in the main unit then place the outer bowl on the base by holding the handle of the bowl in the middle of the appliance. Now twist the handle right side to raise the platform and also lock the bowl. Click sound indicates the outer bowl is locked properly.

6. **Select program:** Press the power button and select the appropriate program button as per your recipe needs.

7. **Remove bowl:** After the end of the program, hold and release the button present on the left side of the motor base. Twist the outer bowl handle clockwise direction to remove.

8. **Remove lid:** Press the lid lock button and twist the lid to open it.

9. **Mix-in:** If needed add your favorite mix-in by making the 1 ½ inch wide hole at the center position of the pint and process it by using the Mix-In function.

Components of Ninja CREAMi

The Ninja CREAMi treat maker comes with four main components. These components include,

1. **Motor Base:** The Ninja CREAMi motor base comes with two independent working motors which take 800 Watt power to work on perfectly. One motor is used to rotate the creameries paddle and another motor to apply the downward force. The motor rotates its full capacity and converts your frozen base into a creamy treat within few seconds.

2. **CREAMi Pints:** CREAMi pints are one kind of plastic container made up of BPA-free material. It is used to hold your ice cream base and used to turn it into ice cream, gelato, sorbet, milkshake, and more. After making ice cream you can store them in the same pint container by placing a CREAMi pint storage lid. There are 3 quantities of CREAMi pints available with this machine. You can also buy extra pints from their official site ninjacreami.com.

3. **Creamerizer Paddle:** The Creamerizer paddle is a dual functioning blade that is used to finely shave your frozen base and also convert it into a smooth creamy base by breaking ice crystals. Before use always check the Creamerizer paddle fit properly without bend or twist.

4. **Outer Bowl:** The outer bowl is used to hold the CREAMi pint with a motor base during processing your frozen base. It comes with an outer bowl lid twisted and locked easily while processing.

Ninja CREAMi Control Panel

The Ninja CREAMi control panel comes with 7 preset functions and one-touch button functions. These functions are mention as follows.

1. **Install Light:** When install light illuminates it indicates that the machine is not fully assembled for use. If the light is in solid color then check paddle is properly install or not. If the light is blinking continuously then check the outer bowl is fixed at its position.

2. **Progress bar:** The Progress bar indicates the progress of the current working program. The four-bar progress led's blinks twice when the current working process is complete.

3. **One-Touch Programs:** The 7 one-touch functions are design to whip your treat within 1 minute to 2 ½ minutes. The speed and length of the programs are varying in each program to convert your frozen treat into the perfect creamy dish. These one-touch programs include,

    Ice Cream: This function is used to convert your dairy and dairy alternative into thick and creamy ice cream. It allows you to customize your ice cream with your favourite flavors and texture.

    Sorbet: Using this function you can easily convert your favorite fruit base with sugary contents into creamy and delightful sorbet.

    Lite Ice Cream: This function is ideal to make healthy sugar-free ice creams with low sugar and low-fat contents. This function is used to make your favorite and healthy ice cream while you are on a keto or paleo-like diet.

    Smoothie Bowl: Smoothie bowls are specially designed to make healthy drinks from fresh or frozen fruits and vegetables with dairy and dairy alternatives.

    Gelato: The gelato function is design to make a custard base. Using this function you can make your favorite dessert and ice cream in Italian style.

    Milkshake: This function is ideal to make your favorite milkshake by combining your favorite ice cream with dairy and mix-in. It creates a delicious thick milkshake within few minutes.

Mix-In: This function is ideal to mix your favorite mix-ins like frozen fruits, chocolate chips, cereals, nuts, candies, and cookies into a creamy base without changing its size and shape. This function works slowly to mix all the ingredients evenly. You get a better result if you add your favorite mix-in at the middle of your CREAMi pint.

4.Re-Spin: This function is used to ensure the texture of the base is creamy or crumbly after using any one preset programs. If the base temperature is very cold then use the Re-spin function.

Features and benefits of Ninja CREAMi

The Ninja CREAMi treat maker is loaded with various features and benefits which are mention as follows.

Dual drive motor: The Ninja CREAMi comes with two individually working motors in which one motor is used to spin the machine paddle and another is used to apply the downward pressure while crushing frozen ice cream base. The motor works on 800Watt power to convert your favourite frozen base into a delicious soft cream.

Multifunctional Appliances: The Ninja CREAMi is a multifunctional appliance that allows you to do various tasks. It makes flavourful ice cream, delicious milkshakes, sorbet, Italian-style gelato, smoothies, and lite cream ice cream by using the one-touch preset button.

Quick processing: Ninja CREAMi takes few minutes to convert the frozen base into cream by churning and breaking down ice crystals to make creamy ice cream, smoothie, gelato, and sorbet.

Make multiple flavors easily: The Ninja CREAMi allows you to make different flavors of ice cream base and frozen these base which is stored into small CREAMi pints. You can easily store these different flavor CREAMi pint bases in the refrigerator. You cannot do these tasks with a bigger ice cream maker.

Easy to operate: The ninja CREAMi treats maker comes with 7 preset functions with an easy one-touch control panel. You just need to place the frozen base and select the appropriate function. Your Ninja CREAMi treats maker ready your frozen treat into cream within few minutes.

Easy to clean: Except dual-motor base all the parts of the ninja CREAMi treat maker are dishwasher safe. You can wash it in the dishwasher or if you don't have a dishwasher then you can wash them with the help of soap and warm water.

Tips

The following tips and tricks help you to make the perfect creamy treat by using Ninja CREAMi treat maker

1. Freeze your ice cream base at least 24 hours into the freezer before placing it into the ice cream churning machine.

2. The soft pieces of Mix-in are broken down and get smaller in size after the mix-in process to avoid the use of little bigger pieces of soft mix-ins.

3. Do not use fresh fruits, spreads, and sauces during ice cream and gelato treats. It may water down your treat. Use frozen fruits or chocolates instead of fresh one.

4. Mix-in spread evenly when only they are added in the center of the pint pot.

5. If adjustable, set your freezer temperature from 9 °F to -7 °F to get the best results. The Ninja CREAMi is designed to work perfectly in this temperature range.

Care and Maintenance

The following step-by-step cleaning instructions will help you to clean your Ninja CREAMi treat maker easily.

1. Unplug the main unit and remove the Creamerizer paddle from the outer bowl.

2. The parts of the Ninja CREAMi treat maker is dishwasher safe. Wash paddle and container lids into the dishwasher. If you don't have a dishwasher then cleans it with soapy and warm water.

3. Before cleaning the outer bowl first remove the paddle. Then remove the grey rubber seal wrapped around the lowest side of the outer bowl. Hand washes the outer lid or cleans it into the dishwasher.

4. Now clean the Dual motor base with the help of a damp cloth. Do not use harsh chemicals or spray to clean the motor base.

5. If you found the liquid drop tapped between the motor bases then raise the platform and clean it using a damp cloth.

Make sure all the parts of the Ninja CREAMi dry thoroughly Before placing it in its original position.

ICE CREAM

Vanilla Ice Cream

Preparation Time: 10 minutes   Cooking Time: 10 minutes   Serve: 6

Nutritional Value (Amount Per Serving)
- Calories 312
- Fat 20.1 g
- Carbohydrates 29 g
- Sugar 27.2 g
- Protein 4.9 g
- Cholesterol 268 mg

Ingredients:
- 6 egg yolks
- 1 tbsp vanilla extract
- 2 cups heavy cream
- 1 cup milk
- ¾ cup sugar
- Pinch of salt

Directions:

- Add egg yolks in a medium saucepan and whisk well. Add sugar, milk, and salt and whisk until smooth. Add cream and whisk well.
- Place the saucepan on the heat and cook over low heat until begins to boil. Stir constantly.
- Remove saucepan from heat and let it cool completely. Stir in vanilla extract.
- Pour base mixture into the creamy pint and cover pint with lid and place in freezer for 24 hours.
- Remove pint from the freezer and take off the lid. Refer to the quick start guide for bowl assembly.
- Press ice cream mode.
- Once processing is done, remove the ice cream and serve.

Chocolate Ice Cream

Preparation Time: 10 minutes   Cooking Time: 10 minutes   Serve: 4

Nutritional Value (Amount Per Serving)
- Calories 232
- Fat 14.1 g
- Carbohydrates 25 g
- Sugar 21.1 g
- Protein 5 g
- Cholesterol 87 mg

Ingredients:
- 1 egg
- 1 cup heavy whipping cream
- 1 cup milk
- 1 tsp vanilla
- ¼ cup cocoa powder
- 6 tbsp sugar

Directions:
- In a bowl, beat egg and sugar for 4-5 minutes. Add cocoa powder, vanilla, milk, and cream and whisk until well blended.
- Pour base mixture into the creamy pint and cover pint with lid and place in freezer for 24 hours.
- Remove pint from the freezer and take off the lid. Refer to the quick start guide for bowl assembly.
- Press ice cream mode.
- Once processing is done, remove the ice cream and serve.

Orange Ice Cream

Preparation Time: 10 minutes   Cooking Time: 10 minutes   Serve: 4

Nutritional Value (Amount Per Serving)
- Calories 465
- Fat 14.9 g
- Carbohydrates 83.8 g
- Sugar 62 g
- Protein 2.9 g
- Cholesterol 55 mg

Ingredients:
- 1 cup orange puree
- ¾ cup milk
- 1 ¼ cups heavy cream
- ½ cup orange juice
- 1 tsp orange extract
- 2 tbsp fresh lemon juice
- ½ cup sugar

Directions:

- In a bowl, beat orange puree and sugar until sugar is dissolved.
- Add lemon juice, orange extract, orange juice, heavy cream, and milk, and whisk well.
- Pour base mixture into the creami pint and cover pint with lid and place in freezer for 24 hours.
- Remove pint from the freezer and take off the lid. Refer to the quick start guide for bowl assembly.
- Press ice cream mode.
- Once processing is done, remove the ice cream and serve.

Strawberry Ice Cream

Preparation Time: 10 minutes   Cooking Time: 10 minutes   Serve: 4

Nutritional Value (Amount Per Serving)
- Calories 356
- Fat 9.3 g
- Carbohydrates 69.3 g
- Sugar 52.7 g
- Protein 1.9 g
- Cholesterol 35 mg

Ingredients:
- 1 cup strawberry puree
- 1 tsp vanilla
- 5 tbsp sugar
- ¾ cup heavy cream
- ½ cup full-fat milk
- Pinch of salt

Directions:

- In a bowl, whisk sugar and milk until sugar is dissolved. Add cream, vanilla, strawberry puree, and salt and whisk well.
- Pour base mixture into the creami pint and cover pint with lid and place in freezer for 24 hours.
- Remove pint from the freezer and take off the lid. Refer to the quick start guide for bowl assembly.
- Press ice cream mode.
- Once processing is done, remove the ice cream and serve.

Cream Cheese Ice Cream

Preparation Time: 10 minutes   Cooking Time: 10 minutes   Serve: 4

Nutritional Value (Amount Per Serving)
- Calories 364
- Fat 22 g
- Carbohydrates 40.6 g
- Sugar 39.3 g
- Protein 3.7 g
- Cholesterol 75 mg

Ingredients:
- 1 cup heavy cream
- 1 tsp vanilla
- 4 oz cream cheese
- ¾ cup sugar
- ½ cup whole milk
- Pinch of salt

Directions:

- Add the cream cheese to a microwave-safe bowl and microwave for 10 seconds.
- Remove bowl from microwave and stir cream cheese well. Add sugar and milk and whisk until sugar is dissolved. Add vanilla, heavy cream, and salt and stir well.
- Pour base mixture into the creami pint and cover pint with lid and place in freezer for 24 hours.
- Remove pint from the freezer and take off the lid. Refer to the quick start guide for bowl assembly.
- Press ice cream mode.
- Once processing is done, remove the ice cream and serve.

Coconut Ice Cream

Preparation Time: 10 minutes   Cooking Time: 10 minutes   Serve: 4

Nutritional Value (Amount Per Serving)
- Calories 324
- Fat 25.5 g
- Carbohydrates 23.4 g
- Sugar 21.3 g
- Protein 4.2 g
- Cholesterol 85 mg

Ingredients:
- 1 egg
- 7.5 oz coconut cream
- ½ cup milk
- 1 cup heavy whipping cream
- 6 tbsp sugar

Directions:

- In a bowl, whisk egg until light. Add sugar and whisk until sugar is well blended.
- Add cream, milk, and coconut cream and stir well.
- Pour base mixture into the creami pint and cover pint with lid and place in freezer for 24 hours.
- Remove pint from the freezer and take off the lid. Refer to the quick start guide for bowl assembly.
- Press ice cream mode.
- Once processing is done, remove the ice cream and serve.

Maple Ice Cream

Preparation Time: 10 minutes   Cooking Time: 10 minutes   Serve: 4

Nutritional Value (Amount Per Serving)
- Calories 227
- Fat 11.6 g
- Carbohydrates 29.9 g
- Sugar 23.6 g
- Protein 2.4 g
- Cholesterol 38 mg

Ingredients:
- ½ cup maple syrup
- ¼ cup heavy whipping cream
- 1 ¼ cups half and half

Directions:
- In a bowl, whisk maple syrup, cream, and a half and a half until well blended.
- Pour base mixture into the creami pint and cover pint with lid and place in freezer for 24 hours.
- Remove pint from the freezer and take off the lid. Refer to the quick start guide for bowl assembly.
- Press ice cream mode.
- Once processing is done, remove the ice cream and serve.

Key Lime Pie Ice Cream

Preparation Time: 10 minutes   Cooking Time: 10 minutes   Serve: 4

Nutritional Value (Amount Per Serving)
- Calories 326
- Fat 16.9 g
- Carbohydrates 42.4 g
- Sugar 31.7 g
- Protein 7.3 g
- Cholesterol 63 mg

Ingredients:
- 1 cup heavy cream
- 1 lime juice
- 1 lime zest
- 6 tbsp key lime juice
- 7 oz can sweeten condensed milk
- 1 cup milk
- Pinch of salt

Directions:

- In a bowl, whisk heavy cream, milk, condensed milk, key lime juice, lime zest, lime juice, and salt until well blended.
- Pour base mixture into the creami pint and cover pint with lid and place in freezer for 24 hours.
- Remove pint from the freezer and take off the lid. Refer to the quick start guide for bowl assembly.
- Press ice cream mode.
- Once processing is done, remove the ice cream and serve.

Pumpkin Pie Ice Cream

Preparation Time: 10 minutes   Cooking Time: 10 minutes   Serve: 6

Nutritional Value (Amount Per Serving)
- Calories 203
- Fat 13.9 g
- Carbohydrates 18.2 g
- Sugar 17.1 g
- Protein 1.9 g
- Cholesterol 50 mg

Ingredients:
- 1 cup whole milk
- 1 ½ tsp vanilla
- 2 cups heavy cream
- ¾ cup brown sugar
- 2 tsp pumpkin pie spice

Directions:
- In a bowl, whisk milk and sugar until sugar is dissolved.
- Add pumpkin pie spice, heavy cream, and vanilla, and whisk well.
- Pour base mixture into the creami pint and cover pint with lid and place in freezer for 24 hours.
- Remove pint from the freezer and take off the lid. Refer to the quick start guide for bowl assembly.
- Press ice cream mode.
- Once processing is done, remove the ice cream and serve.

Pineapple Coconut Ice Cream

Preparation Time: 10 minutes   Cooking Time: 10 minutes   Serve: 6

Nutritional Value (Amount Per Serving)
- Calories 284
- Fat 19.9 g
- Carbohydrates 23.9 g
- Sugar 21.4 g
- Protein 3.9 g
- Cholesterol 66 mg

Ingredients:
- ½ cup shredded coconut
- 7 oz pineapple puree
- 7 oz condensed milk
- 2 cups heavy whipping cream

Directions:
- In a bowl, whisk cream, condensed milk, pineapple puree, and shredded coconut until well blended.
- Pour base mixture into the creami pint and cover pint with lid and place in freezer for 24 hours.
- Remove pint from the freezer and take off the lid. Refer to the quick start guide for bowl assembly.
- Press ice cream mode.
- Once processing is done, remove the ice cream and serve.

Pumpkin Ice Cream

Preparation Time: 10 minutes   Cooking Time: 10 minutes   Serve: 4

Nutritional Value (Amount Per Serving)
- Calories 267
- Fat 14.9 g
- Carbohydrates 29.9 g
- Sugar 27.9 g
- Protein 4.8 g
- Cholesterol 56 mg

Ingredients:
- 4 oz heavy whipping cream
- ½ tsp vanilla extract
- ½ tsp pumpkin pie spice
- 6 tbsp pumpkin puree
- 7 oz condensed milk

Directions:
- In a bowl, whisk milk, pumpkin puree, pumpkin pie spice, vanilla, and cream until well blended.
- Pour base mixture into the creami pint and cover pint with lid and place in freezer for 24 hours.
- Remove pint from the freezer and take off the lid. Refer to the quick start guide for bowl assembly.
- Press ice cream mode.
- Once processing is done, remove the ice cream and serve.

Mango Ice Cream

Preparation Time: 10 minutes   Cooking Time: 10 minutes   Serve: 4

Nutritional Value (Amount Per Serving)
- Calories 492
- Fat 49.9 g
- Carbohydrates 12.9 g
- Sugar 11.7 g
- Protein 0.6 g
- Cholesterol 0 mg

Ingredients:
- 1 ½ cups mango puree
- ½ tsp vanilla
- 7 oz full-fat coconut cream
- 1 tbsp maple syrup
- 1 tbsp milk

Directions:

- In a bowl, whisk mango puree, milk, maple syrup, coconut cream, and vanilla until well blended.
- Pour base mixture into the creami pint and cover pint with lid and place in freezer for 24 hours.
- Remove pint from the freezer and take off the lid. Refer to the quick start guide for bowl assembly.
- Press ice cream mode.
- Once processing is done, remove the ice cream and serve.

Peanut Butter Ice Cream

Preparation Time: 10 minutes   Cooking Time: 10 minutes   Serve: 4

Nutritional Value (Amount Per Serving)
- Calories 358
- Fat 23.6 g
- Carbohydrates 31 g
- Sugar 28.5 g
- Protein 8.6 g
- Cholesterol 58 mg

Ingredients:
- 1 cup heavy cream
- ¼ cup smooth peanut butter
- 7 oz condensed milk

Directions:
- In a bowl, whisk condensed milk, peanut butter, and heavy cream until well blended.
- Pour base mixture into the creami pint and cover pint with lid and place in freezer for 24 hours.
- Remove pint from the freezer and take off the lid. Refer to the quick start guide for bowl assembly.
- Press ice cream mode.
- Once processing is done, remove the ice cream and serve.

Chocolate Peanut Butter Ice Cream

Preparation Time: 10 minutes   Cooking Time: 10 minutes   Serve: 4

Nutritional Value (Amount Per Serving)
- Calories 259
- Fat 17.2 g
- Carbohydrates 24.2 g
- Sugar 18.2 g
- Protein 4.3 g
- Cholesterol 58 mg

Ingredients:
- 1 cup heavy cream
- 1 tsp vanilla extract
- ¾ cup half and half
- 6 tbsp sugar
- ½ cup chocolate peanut butter

Directions:

- In a bowl, beat chocolate peanut butter and sugar until smooth. Add half and half, vanilla, and heavy cream, and whisk until well combined.
- Pour base mixture into the creami pint and cover pint with lid and place in freezer for 24 hours.
- Remove pint from the freezer and take off the lid. Refer to the quick start guide for bowl assembly.
- Press ice cream mode.
- Once processing is done, remove the ice cream and serve.

Peach Ice Cream

Preparation Time: 10 minutes   Cooking Time: 10 minutes   Serve: 4

Nutritional Value (Amount Per Serving)
- Calories 135
- Fat 5.9 g
- Carbohydrates 21 g
- Sugar 20.5 g
- Protein 1 g
- Cholesterol 22 mg

Ingredients:
- ½ cup peach puree
- ¼ tsp vanilla
- ¼ cup milk
- ½ cup heavy cream
- 6 tbsp sugar

Directions:
- In a bowl, whisk sugar and milk until sugar is dissolved. Add cream, vanilla, and peach puree and whisk until well blended.
- Pour base mixture into the creami pint and cover pint with lid and place in freezer for 24 hours.
- Remove pint from the freezer and take off the lid. Refer to the quick start guide for bowl assembly.
- Press ice cream mode.
- Once processing is done, remove the ice cream and serve.

Coffee Ice Cream

Preparation Time: 10 minutes   Cooking Time: 10 minutes   Serve: 4

Nutritional Value (Amount Per Serving)
- Calories 159
- Fat 10.5 g
- Carbohydrates 14.2 g
- Sugar 13.6 g
- Protein 2.4 g
- Cholesterol 39 mg

Ingredients:
- 2 tsp instant coffee powder
- ½ tsp vanilla extract
- 3.5 oz condensed milk
- ¾ cup heavy whipping cream
- 1 tbsp water

Directions:

- In a bowl, add coffee powder and water and stir until coffee powder is dissolved.
- Add cream, condensed milk, and vanilla extract and whisk until well blended.
- Pour base mixture into the creami pint and cover pint with lid and place in freezer for 24 hours.
- Remove pint from the freezer and take off the lid. Refer to the quick start guide for bowl assembly.
- Press ice cream mode.
- Once processing is done, remove the ice cream and serve.

Avocado Ice Cream

Preparation Time: 10 minutes   Cooking Time: 10 minutes   Serve: 4

Nutritional Value (Amount Per Serving)
- Calories 201
- Fat 10.1 g
- Carbohydrates 25.6 g
- Sugar 23 g
- Protein 3.6 g
- Cholesterol 34 mg

Ingredients:
- 1 avocado puree
- ½ cup heavy cream
- ½ lime juice
- ½ lime zest
- ½ cup condensed milk

Directions:
- In a bowl, whisk avocado puree, cream, lime juice, lime zest, and condensed milk until well blended.
- Pour base mixture into the creami pint and cover pint with lid and place in freezer for 24 hours.
- Remove pint from the freezer and take off the lid. Refer to the quick start guide for bowl assembly.
- Press ice cream mode.
- Once processing is done, remove the ice cream and serve.

Almond milk Ice Cream

Preparation Time: 10 minutes   Cooking Time: 10 minutes   Serve: 4

Nutritional Value (Amount Per Serving)
- Calories 193
- Fat 15.1 g
- Carbohydrates 14 g
- Sugar 7.8 g
- Protein 3.3 g
- Cholesterol 0 mg

Ingredients:
- ½ cup cashews, soak in water overnight
- 2 tbsp maple syrup
- ½ cup almond milk

Directions:
- Add cashews, maple syrup, and almond milk in a blender and blend until smooth.
- Pour base mixture into the creami pint and cover pint with lid and place in freezer for 24 hours.
- Remove pint from the freezer and take off the lid. Refer to the quick start guide for bowl assembly.
- Press ice cream mode.
- Once processing is done, remove the ice cream and serve.

Lemon Ice Cream

Preparation Time: 10 minutes   Cooking Time: 10 minutes   Serve: 4

Nutritional Value (Amount Per Serving)
- Calories 275
- Fat 17.5 g
- Carbohydrates 28.5 g
- Sugar 27.2 g
- Protein 2.2 g
- Cholesterol 64 mg

Ingredients:
- 1 ½ cups heavy cream
- 1 tsp lemon extract
- ½ cup lemon juice
- ½ cup sugar
- ½ cup milk

Directions:
- In a bowl, whisk heavy cream, lemon extract, lemon juice, sugar, and milk until sugar is dissolved.
- Pour base mixture into the creami pint and cover pint with lid and place in freezer for 24 hours.
- Remove pint from the freezer and take off the lid. Refer to the quick start guide for bowl assembly.
- Press ice cream mode.
- Once processing is done, remove the ice cream and serve.

Coconut Maple Ice Cream

Preparation Time: 10 minutes   Cooking Time: 10 minutes   Serve: 5

Nutritional Value (Amount Per Serving)

- Calories 217
- Fat 19.3 g
- Carbohydrates 10.1 g
- Sugar 5.6 g
- Protein 4.9 g
- Cholesterol 0 mg

Ingredients:

- 7 oz can coconut milk
- ¼ tsp coconut extract
- 2 tbsp maple syrup
- 6 tbsp almond butter

Directions:

- In a bowl, whisk almond butter, maple syrup, coconut extract, and coconut milk until well blended.
- Pour base mixture into the creami pint and cover pint with lid and place in freezer for 24 hours.
- Remove pint from the freezer and take off the lid. Refer to the quick start guide for bowl assembly.
- Press ice cream mode.
- Once processing is done, remove the ice cream and serve.

Cookie Ice Cream

Preparation Time: 10 minutes   Cooking Time: 10 minutes   Serve: 6

Nutritional Value (Amount Per Serving)
- Calories 392
- Fat 23.1 g
- Carbohydrates 41.5 g
- Sugar 34.2 g
- Protein 5.9 g
- Cholesterol 268 mg

Ingredients:
- 6 egg yolks
- 1 tbsp vanilla extract
- 2 cups heavy cream
- 1 cup milk
- ¾ cup sugar
- Pinch of salt
- 3 chocolate sandwich cookies, broken

Directions:

- Add egg yolks in a medium saucepan and whisk well. Add sugar, milk, and salt and whisk until smooth. Add cream and whisk well.
- Place the saucepan on the heat and cook over low heat until begins to boil. Stir constantly.
- Remove saucepan from heat and let it cool completely. Stir in vanilla extract.
- Pour base mixture into the creami pint and cover pint with lid and place in freezer for 24 hours.
- Remove pint from the freezer and take off the lid. Refer to the quick start guide for bowl assembly.
- Press ice cream mode.
- Once processing is done, add cookies then press mix-in mode.
- Once processing is done, remove the ice cream and serve.

Chocolate Almond Ice Cream

Preparation Time: 10 minutes   Cooking Time: 10 minutes   Serve: 4

Nutritional Value (Amount Per Serving)
- Calories 277
- Fat 17.2 g
- Carbohydrates 28.8 g
- Sugar 23.9 g
- Protein 6 g
- Cholesterol 88 mg

Ingredients:
- 1 egg
- 1 cup heavy whipping cream
- 1 cup milk
- 1 tsp vanilla
- ¼ cup cocoa powder
- 6 tbsp sugar
- 2 tbsp almonds, chopped
- 2 tbsp chocolate chips

Directions:
- In a bowl, beat egg and sugar for 4-5 minutes. Add cocoa powder, vanilla, milk, and cream and whisk until well blended.
- Pour base mixture into the creami pint and cover pint with lid and place in freezer for 24 hours.
- Remove pint from the freezer and take off the lid. Refer to the quick start guide for bowl assembly.
- Press ice cream mode.
- Once processing is done, add almonds and chocolate chips then press mix-in mode.
- Once processing is done, remove the ice cream and serve.

Choco Chip Orange Ice Cream

Preparation Time: 10 minutes   Cooking Time: 10 minutes   Serve: 4

Nutritional Value (Amount Per Serving)
- Calories 521
- Fat 18.1 g
- Carbohydrates 90.1 g
- Sugar 67.4 g
- Protein 3.7 g
- Cholesterol 58 mg

Ingredients:
- 1 cup orange puree
- ¾ cup milk
- 1 ¼ cups heavy cream
- ½ cup orange juice
- 1 tsp orange extract
- 2 tbsp fresh lemon juice
- ½ cup sugar
- ¼ cup chocolate chips

Directions:
- In a bowl, beat orange puree and sugar until sugar is dissolved.
- Add lemon juice, orange extract, orange juice, heavy cream, and milk, and whisk well.
- Pour base mixture into the creami pint and cover pint with lid and place in freezer for 24 hours.
- Remove pint from the freezer and take off the lid. Refer to the quick start guide for bowl assembly.
- Press ice cream mode.
- Once processing is done, add chocolate chips then press mix-in mode.
- Once processing is done, remove the ice cream and serve.

Chocolate Chip Ice Cream

Preparation Time: 10 minutes   Cooking Time: 10 minutes   Serve: 4

Nutritional Value (Amount Per Serving)
- Calories 288
- Fat 17.3 g
- Carbohydrates 31.2 g
- Sugar 26.5 g
- Protein 5.8 g
- Cholesterol 89 mg

Ingredients:
- 1 egg
- 1 cup heavy whipping cream
- 1 cup milk
- 1 tsp vanilla
- ¼ cup cocoa powder
- 6 tbsp sugar
- 4 tbsp chocolate chips

Directions:

- In a bowl, beat egg and sugar for 4-5 minutes. Add cocoa powder, vanilla, milk, and cream and whisk until well blended.
- Pour base mixture into the creami pint and cover pint with lid and place in freezer for 24 hours.
- Remove pint from the freezer and take off the lid. Refer to the quick start guide for bowl assembly.
- Press ice cream mode.
- Once processing is done, add chocolate chips then press mix-in mode.
- Once processing is done, remove the ice cream and serve.

Death by Chocolate Ice Cream

Preparation Time: 10 minutes   Cooking Time: 10 minutes   Serve: 4

Nutritional Value (Amount Per Serving)
- Calories 381
- Fat 21.8 g
- Carbohydrates 42.4 g
- Sugar 32.6 g
- Protein 7.4 g
- Cholesterol 92 mg

Ingredients:
- 1 egg
- 1 cup heavy whipping cream
- 1 cup milk
- 1 tsp vanilla
- ¼ cup cocoa powder
- 6 tbsp sugar
- 2 tbsp almonds, chopped
- 2 tbsp chocolate chips
- 2 tbsp brownie chunks
- 2 tbsp chocolate chips

Directions:
- In a bowl, beat egg and sugar for 4-5 minutes. Add cocoa powder, vanilla, milk, and cream and whisk until well blended.
- Pour base mixture into the creami pint and cover pint with lid and place in freezer for 24 hours.
- Remove pint from the freezer and take off the lid. Refer to the quick start guide for bowl assembly.
- Press ice cream mode.
- Once processing is done, add brownie chunks and chocolate chips then press mix-in mode.
- Once processing is done, remove the ice cream and serve.

Choco Chip Cookie Dough Ice Cream

Preparation Time: 10 minutes   Cooking Time: 10 minutes   Serve: 6

Nutritional Value (Amount Per Serving)
- Calories 330
- Fat 21.1 g
- Carbohydrates 31 g
- Sugar 28.8 g
- Protein 5.1 g
- Cholesterol 269 mg

Ingredients:
- 6 egg yolks
- 1 tbsp vanilla extract
- 2 cups heavy cream
- 1 cup milk
- ¾ cup sugar
- Pinch of salt
- 1 tbsp chocolate chips
- 1/4 cup frozen cookie dough chunks

Directions:

- Add egg yolks in a medium saucepan and whisk well. Add sugar, milk, and salt and whisk until smooth. Add cream and whisk well.
- Place the saucepan on the heat and cook over low heat until begins to boil. Stir constantly.
- Remove saucepan from heat and let it cool completely.
- Pour base mixture into the creami pint and cover pint with lid and place in freezer for 24 hours.
- Remove pint from the freezer and take off the lid. Refer to the quick start guide for bowl assembly.
- Press ice cream mode.
- Once processing is done, add chocolate chips and frozen cookie dough chunks then press mix-in mode.
- Once processing is done, remove the ice cream and serve.

Maple Walnut Ice Cream

Preparation Time: 10 minutes   Cooking Time: 10 minutes   Serve: 4

Nutritional Value (Amount Per Serving)
- Calories 278
- Fat 16.2 g
- Carbohydrates 30.8 g
- Sugar 23.8 g
- Protein 4.3 g
- Cholesterol 38 mg

Ingredients:
- ½ cup maple syrup
- ¼ cup heavy whipping cream
- 1 ¼ cups half and half
- 1 tsp maple extract
- ¼ cup walnut, chopped

Directions:
- In a bowl, whisk maple syrup, cream, maple extract, and a half and a half until well blended.
- Pour base mixture into the creami pint and cover pint with lid and place in freezer for 24 hours.
- Remove pint from the freezer and take off the lid. Refer to the quick start guide for bowl assembly.
- Press ice cream mode.
- Once processing is done, add walnut then press mix-in mode.
- Once processing is done, remove the ice cream and serve.

Coffee Chocó Chip Ice Cream

Preparation Time: 10 minutes   Cooking Time: 10 minutes   Serve: 4

Nutritional Value (Amount Per Serving)
- Calories 215
- Fat 13.6 g
- Carbohydrates 20.4 g
- Sugar 19 g
- Protein 3.2 g
- Cholesterol 42 mg

Ingredients:
- 2 tsp instant coffee powder
- ½ tsp vanilla extract
- 3.5 oz condensed milk
- ¾ cup heavy whipping cream
- 1 tbsp water
- ¼ cup chocolate chips

Directions:
- In a bowl, add coffee powder and water and stir until coffee powder is dissolved.
- Add cream, condensed milk, and vanilla extract and whisk until well blended.
- Pour base mixture into the creami pint and cover pint with lid and place in freezer for 24 hours.
- Remove pint from the freezer and take off the lid. Refer to the quick start guide for bowl assembly.
- Press ice cream mode.
- Once processing is done, add chocolate chips then press mix-in mode.
- Once processing is done, remove the ice cream and serve.

Pistachio Ice Cream

Preparation Time: 10 minutes   Cooking Time: 10 minutes   Serve: 6

Nutritional Value (Amount Per Serving)
- Calories 326
- Fat 21.3 g
- Carbohydrates 29.7 g
- Sugar 27.4 g
- Protein 8.7 g
- Cholesterol 268 mg

Ingredients:
- 6 egg yolks
- 1 tbsp almond extract
- 2 cups heavy cream
- 1 cup milk
- ¾ cup sugar
- Pinch of salt
- ¼ cup pistachio, chopped

Directions:
- Add egg yolks in a medium saucepan and whisk well. Add sugar, milk, and salt and whisk until smooth. Add cream and whisk well.
- Place the saucepan on the heat and cook over low heat until begins to boil. Stir constantly.
- Remove saucepan from heat and let it cool completely. Stir in almond extract.
- Pour base mixture into the creami pint and cover pint with lid and place in freezer for 24 hours.
- Remove pint from the freezer and take off the lid. Refer to the quick start guide for bowl assembly.
- Press ice cream mode.
- Once processing is done, add pistachio then press mix-in mode.
- Once processing is done, remove the ice cream and serve.

Raisin Rum Ice Cream

Preparation Time: 10 minutes   Cooking Time: 10 minutes   Serve: 6

Nutritional Value (Amount Per Serving)
- Calories 329
- Fat 20.2 g
- Carbohydrates 33.5 g
- Sugar 30.6 g
- Protein 5 g
- Cholesterol 268 mg

Ingredients:
- 6 egg yolks
- 1 tbsp rum extract
- 2 cups heavy cream
- 1 cup milk
- ¾ cup sugar
- Pinch of salt
- ¼ cup raisins, soak in hot water

Directions:

- Add egg yolks in a medium saucepan and whisk well. Add sugar, milk, and salt and whisk until smooth. Add cream and whisk well.
- Place the saucepan on the heat and cook over low heat until begins to boil. Stir constantly.
- Remove saucepan from heat and let it cool completely. Stir in rum extract.
- Pour base mixture into the creami pint and cover pint with lid and place in freezer for 24 hours.
- Remove pint from the freezer and take off the lid. Refer to the quick start guide for bowl assembly.
- Press ice cream mode.
- Once processing is done, add raisins then press mix-in mode.
- Once processing is done, remove the ice cream and serve.

Chocolate Toffee Crunch Ice Cream

Preparation Time: 10 minutes   Cooking Time: 10 minutes   Serve: 4

Nutritional Value (Amount Per Serving)
- Calories 261
- Fat 15.3 g
- Carbohydrates 29.4 g
- Sugar 23.4 g
- Protein 5.3 g
- Cholesterol 0 mg

Ingredients:
- 1 egg
- 1 cup heavy whipping cream
- 1 cup milk
- 1 tsp vanilla
- ¼ cup cocoa powder
- 6 tbsp sugar
- ¼ cup chocolate toffee bar, broken

Directions:
- In a bowl, beat egg and sugar for 4-5 minutes. Add cocoa powder, vanilla, milk, and cream and whisk until well blended.
- Pour base mixture into the creami pint and cover pint with lid and place in freezer for 24 hours.
- Remove pint from the freezer and take off the lid. Refer to the quick start guide for bowl assembly.
- Press ice cream mode.
- Once processing is done, add a chocolate toffee bar then press mix-in mode.
- Once processing is done, remove the ice cream and serve.

Chocolate Cashew Ice Cream

Preparation Time: 10 minutes   Cooking Time: 10 minutes   Serve: 4

Nutritional Value (Amount Per Serving)
- Calories 281
- Fat 18.1 g
- Carbohydrates 27.8 g
- Sugar 21.5 g
- Protein 6.3 g
- Cholesterol 87 mg

Ingredients:
- 1 egg
- 1 cup heavy whipping cream
- 1 cup milk
- 1 tsp vanilla
- ¼ cup cocoa powder
- 6 tbsp sugar
- ¼ cup cashews, roasted & chopped

Directions:
- In a bowl, beat egg and sugar for 4-5 minutes. Add cocoa powder, vanilla, milk, and cream and whisk until well blended.
- Pour base mixture into the creami pint and cover pint with lid and place in freezer for 24 hours.
- Remove pint from the freezer and take off the lid. Refer to the quick start guide for bowl assembly.
- Press ice cream mode.
- Once processing is done, add cashews then press mix-in mode.
- Once processing is done, remove the ice cream and serve.

Chocolate Caramel Ice Cream

Preparation Time: 10 minutes   Cooking Time: 10 minutes   Serve: 4

Nutritional Value (Amount Per Serving)
- Calories 247
- Fat 15.1 g
- Carbohydrates 26.1 g
- Sugar 22.1 g
- Protein 5.1 g
- Cholesterol 88 mg

Ingredients:
- 1 egg
- 1 cup heavy whipping cream
- 1 cup milk
- 1 tsp vanilla
- ¼ cup cocoa powder
- 6 tbsp sugar
- ¼ cup chocolate caramel candy, broken

Directions:
- In a bowl, beat egg and sugar for 4-5 minutes. Add cocoa powder, vanilla, milk, and cream and whisk until well blended.
- Pour base mixture into the creami pint and cover pint with lid and place in freezer for 24 hours.
- Remove pint from the freezer and take off the lid. Refer to the quick start guide for bowl assembly.
- Press ice cream mode.
- Once processing is done, add chocolate caramel candy then press mix-in mode.
- Once processing is done, remove the ice cream and serve.

Almond Coconut Ice Cream

Preparation Time: 10 minutes   Cooking Time: 10 minutes   Serve: 4

Nutritional Value (Amount Per Serving)
- Calories 350
- Fat 27.7 g
- Carbohydrates 24.3 g
- Sugar 21.5 g
- Protein 5.2 g
- Cholesterol 85 mg

Ingredients:
- 1 egg
- 7.5 oz coconut cream
- ½ cup milk
- 1 cup heavy whipping cream
- 6 tbsp sugar
- 3 tbsp almonds, chopped

Directions:

- In a bowl, whisk egg until light. Add sugar and whisk until sugar is well blended.
- Add cream, milk, and coconut cream and stir well.
- Pour base mixture into the creami pint and cover pint with lid and place in freezer for 24 hours.
- Remove pint from the freezer and take off the lid. Refer to the quick start guide for bowl assembly.
- Press ice cream mode.
- Once processing is done, add almonds then press mix-in mode.
- Once processing is done, remove the ice cream and serve.

Chocolate Cookie Ice Cream

Preparation Time: 10 minutes   Cooking Time: 10 minutes   Serve: 4

Nutritional Value (Amount Per Serving)
- Calories 352
- Fat 18.6 g
- Carbohydrates 43.8 g
- Sugar 31.6 g
- Protein 6.5 g
- Cholesterol 87 mg

Ingredients:
- 1 egg
- 1 cup heavy whipping cream
- 1 cup milk
- 1 tsp vanilla
- ¼ cup cocoa powder
- 6 tbsp sugar
- 3 chocolate sandwich cookies, broken

Directions:
- In a bowl, beat egg and sugar for 4-5 minutes. Add cocoa powder, vanilla, milk, and cream and whisk until well blended.
- Pour base mixture into the creami pint and cover pint with lid and place in freezer for 24 hours.
- Remove pint from the freezer and take off the lid. Refer to the quick start guide for bowl assembly.
- Press ice cream mode.
- Once processing is done, add chocolate sandwich cookies then press mix-in mode.
- Once processing is done, remove the ice cream and serve.

MILKSHAKE

Nutella Milkshake

Preparation Time: 5 minutes   Cooking Time: 5 minutes   Serve: 1

Nutritional Value (Amount Per Serving)
- Calories 234
- Fat 11.9 g
- Carbohydrates 26.7 g
- Sugar 23.4 g
- Protein 5 g
- Cholesterol 34 mg

Ingredients:
- 1/3 cup Nutella
- ¼ cup milk
- 1 cup vanilla ice cream

Directions:
- Add all ingredients into the creami pint. Refer to the quick start guide for bowl assembly.
- Press milkshake mode.
- Once processing is done, remove the milkshake and serve.

Strawberry Milkshake

Preparation Time: 5 minutes   Cooking Time: 5 minutes   Serve: 2

Nutritional Value (Amount Per Serving)
- Calories 127
- Fat 4.3 g
- Carbohydrates 20 g
- Sugar 17.3 g
- Protein 2.5 g
- Cholesterol 17 mg

Ingredients:
- ¼ lb strawberries, chopped
- ¼ cup milk
- ½ tsp vanilla extract
- 1 cup vanilla ice cream
- 1 tbsp sugar

Directions:
- Add all ingredients into the creami pint. Refer to the quick start guide for bowl assembly.
- Press milkshake mode.
- Once processing is done, remove the milkshake and serve.

Coffee Milkshake

Preparation Time: 5 minutes   Cooking Time: 5 minutes   Serve: 2

Nutritional Value (Amount Per Serving)
- Calories 332
- Fat 16.6 g
- Carbohydrates 39.5 g
- Sugar 32.2 g
- Protein 8.6 g
- Cholesterol 66 mg

Ingredients:
- 4 scoops of vanilla ice cream
- 2 tbsp cocoa powder
- 2 tbsp instant coffee granules
- ¾ cup milk

Directions:
- Add all ingredients into the creami pint. Refer to the quick start guide for bowl assembly.
- Press milkshake mode.
- Once processing is done, remove the milkshake and serve.

Banana Milkshake

Preparation Time: 5 minutes   Cooking Time: 5 minutes   Serve: 1

Nutritional Value (Amount Per Serving)
- Calories 364
- Fat 10.7 g
- Carbohydrates 59.5 g
- Sugar 40.6 g
- Protein 12 g
- Cholesterol 33 mg

Ingredients:
- 1 ripe banana, cut into pieces
- 1 tsp vanilla
- 1 tbsp sugar
- 1 cup milk
- 2/3 cup crushed ice

Directions:
- Add all ingredients into the creami pint. Refer to the quick start guide for bowl assembly.
- Press milkshake mode.
- Once processing is done, remove the milkshake and serve.

Chocolate Banana Milkshake

Preparation Time: 5 minutes   Cooking Time: 5 minutes   Serve: 1

Nutritional Value (Amount Per Serving)
- Calories 372
- Fat 5.6 g
- Carbohydrates 76.2 g
- Sugar 61.7 g
- Protein 9.6 g
- Cholesterol 20 mg

Ingredients:
- 1 ripe banana, chopped
- ½ tsp vanilla
- 3 tbsp sugar
- 1 tsp cocoa powder
- 1 cup milk

Directions:
- Add all ingredients into the creami pint. Refer to the quick start guide for bowl assembly.
- Press milkshake mode.
- Once processing is done, remove the milkshake and serve.

Vanilla Milkshake

Preparation Time: 5 minutes   Cooking Time: 5 minutes   Serve: 2

Nutritional Value (Amount Per Serving)
- Calories 219
- Fat 14 g
- Carbohydrates 18.7 g
- Sugar 14.2 g
- Protein 4.1 g
- Cholesterol 51 mg

Ingredients:
- 2 cups vanilla ice cream
- ½ tsp vanilla
- ½ cup half and half

Directions:
- Add all ingredients into the creami pint. Refer to the quick start guide for bowl assembly.
- Press milkshake mode.
- Once processing is done, remove the milkshake and serve.

Chocolate Milkshake

Preparation Time: 5 minutes   Cooking Time: 5 minutes   Serve: 2

Nutritional Value (Amount Per Serving)
- Calories 365
- Fat 12.7 g
- Carbohydrates 56 g
- Sugar 50.1 g
- Protein 11.3 g
- Cholesterol 49 mg

Ingredients:
- 2 scoops of ice cream
- ¼ cup hot water
- ¼ cup sugar
- 2 tbsp cocoa powder
- 2 cups milk

Directions:

- Add all ingredients into the creami pint. Refer to the quick start guide for bowl assembly.
- Press milkshake mode.
- Once processing is done, remove the milkshake and serve.

Peanut Butter Milkshake

Preparation Time: 5 minutes   Cooking Time: 5 minutes   Serve: 1

Nutritional Value (Amount Per Serving)
- Calories 887
- Fat 70.9 g
- Carbohydrates 39.4 g
- Sugar 24.6 g
- Protein 37.4 g
- Cholesterol 25 mg

Ingredients:
- ½ cup milk
- ½ cup peanut butter
- ½ cup vanilla ice cream

Directions:
- Add all ingredients into the creami pint. Refer to the quick start guide for bowl assembly.
- Press milkshake mode.
- Once processing is done, remove the milkshake and serve.

Pumpkin Pie Milkshake

Preparation Time: 5 minutes   Cooking Time: 5 minutes   Serve: 2

Nutritional Value (Amount Per Serving)
- Calories 228
- Fat 10 g
- Carbohydrates 28.9 g
- Sugar 21.7 g
- Protein 7.1 g
- Cholesterol 39 mg

Ingredients:
- 1 tbsp pumpkin pie spice
- ½ cup pumpkin puree
- 1 cup milk
- 2 cups vanilla ice cream

Directions:
- Add all ingredients into the creami pint. Refer to the quick start guide for bowl assembly.
- Press milkshake mode.
- Once processing is done, remove the milkshake and serve.

Choco Banana Peanut Butter Milkshake

Preparation Time: 5 minutes   Cooking Time: 5 minutes   Serve: 2

Nutritional Value (Amount Per Serving)
- Calories 712
- Fat 48.6 g
- Carbohydrates 61.5 g
- Sugar 41.5 g
- Protein 14 g
- Cholesterol 40 mg

Ingredients:
- 1 banana, sliced
- 3 tbsp creamy peanut butter
- ½ cup coconut milk
- 2 cups peanut butter ice cream

Directions:

- Add all ingredients into the creami pint. Refer to the quick start guide for bowl assembly.
- Press milkshake mode.
- Once processing is done, remove the milkshake and serve.

Berry Cheesecake Milkshake

Preparation Time: 5 minutes   Cooking Time: 5 minutes   Serve: 2

Nutritional Value (Amount Per Serving)
- Calories 280
- Fat 17.3 g
- Carbohydrates 25 g
- Sugar 19.4 g
- Protein 7.6 g
- Cholesterol 60 mg

Ingredients:
- 2 oz cream cheese
- 1/3 cup blackberries
- ½ cup strawberries, chopped
- ¼ cup blueberries
- ¾ cup milk
- 1 ½ cups vanilla ice cream

Directions:
- Add all ingredients into the creami pint. Refer to the quick start guide for bowl assembly.
- Press milkshake mode.
- Once processing is done, remove the milkshake and serve.

Blackberry Milkshake

Preparation Time: 5 minutes   Cooking Time: 5 minutes   Serve: 2

Nutritional Value (Amount Per Serving)
- Calories 246
- Fat 8.6 g
- Carbohydrates 38.9 g
- Sugar 33.2 g
- Protein 5.4 g
- Cholesterol 34 mg

Ingredients:
- 1 cup blackberries
- 1 ½ tbsp honey
- ½ cup milk
- 2 cups vanilla ice cream

Directions:
- Add all ingredients into the creami pint. Refer to the quick start guide for bowl assembly.
- Press milkshake mode.
- Once processing is done, remove the milkshake and serve.

Blueberry Milkshake

Preparation Time: 5 minutes   Cooking Time: 5 minutes   Serve: 2

Nutritional Value (Amount Per Serving)
- Calories 240
- Fat 9.8 g
- Carbohydrates 32.7 g
- Sugar 26.7 g
- Protein 6.9 g
- Cholesterol 39 mg

Ingredients:
- 2 cups vanilla ice cream
- ¼ tsp cinnamon
- 1 cup milk
- 1 cup blueberries

Directions:

- Add all ingredients into the creami pint. Refer to the quick start guide for bowl assembly.
- Press milkshake mode.
- Once processing is done, remove the milkshake and serve.

White Chocolate Milkshake

Preparation Time: 5 minutes   Cooking Time: 5 minutes   Serve: 1

Nutritional Value (Amount Per Serving)
- Calories 734
- Fat 37.2 g
- Carbohydrates 87 g
- Sugar 77.2 g
- Protein 12.7 g
- Cholesterol 121 mg

Ingredients:
- 2 tbsp white chocolate spread
- ¼ cup milk
- 4 scoops of vanilla ice cream

Directions:
- Add all ingredients into the creami pint. Refer to the quick start guide for bowl assembly.
- Press milkshake mode.
- Once processing is done, remove the milkshake and serve.

Coconut Mango Milkshake

Preparation Time: 5 minutes   Cooking Time: 5 minutes   Serve: 2

Nutritional Value (Amount Per Serving)
- Calories 313
- Fat 20.8 g
- Carbohydrates 30.3 g
- Sugar 25.5 g
- Protein 4.1 g
- Cholesterol 27 mg

Ingredients:
- 1 ½ cups vanilla ice cream
- 1 tbsp sugar
- ½ cup frozen mango
- ½ cup coconut milk

Directions:
- Add all ingredients into the creami pint. Refer to the quick start guide for bowl assembly.
- Press milkshake mode.
- Once processing is done, remove the milkshake and serve.

Mango Milkshake

Preparation Time: 5 minutes   Cooking Time: 5 minutes   Serve: 2

Nutritional Value (Amount Per Serving)
- Calories 190
- Fat 9.6 g
- Carbohydrates 25.2 g
- Sugar 21.8 g
- Protein 3 g
- Cholesterol 3 mg

Ingredients:
- ¾ cup fresh mangoes, chopped
- 2 tsp sugar
- ½ cup cashew milk

Directions:
- Add all ingredients into the creami pint. Refer to the quick start guide for bowl assembly.
- Press milkshake mode.
- Once processing is done, remove the milkshake and serve.

Chocolate Protein Shake

Preparation Time: 5 minutes   Cooking Time: 5 minutes   Serve: 1

Nutritional Value (Amount Per Serving)
- Calories 268
- Fat 13.3 g
- Carbohydrates 27.2 g
- Sugar 11.8 g
- Protein 16.8 g
- Cholesterol 20 mg

Ingredients:
- 1 scoop chocolate protein powder
- 1 tbsp cocoa powder
- 1 tbsp creamy peanut butter
- 1 cup unsweetened almond milk
- ½ cup banana, sliced

Directions:
- Add all ingredients into the creami pint. Refer to the quick start guide for bowl assembly.
- Press milkshake mode.
- Once processing is done, remove the milkshake and serve.

Caramel Milkshake

Preparation Time: 5 minutes   Cooking Time: 5 minutes   Serve: 1

Nutritional Value (Amount Per Serving)
- Calories 370
- Fat 13 g
- Carbohydrates 57 g
- Sugar 26.5 g
- Protein 8.1 g
- Cholesterol 54 mg

Ingredients:
- ½ cup milk
- 1 ½ cups vanilla ice cream
- 2 tbsp caramel sauce

Directions:
- Add all ingredients into the creami pint. Refer to the quick start guide for bowl assembly.
- Press milkshake mode.
- Once processing is done, remove the milkshake and serve.

Dulce de Leche Milkshake

Preparation Time: 5 minutes   Cooking Time: 5 minutes   Serve: 1

Nutritional Value (Amount Per Serving)
- Calories 377
- Fat 14.5 g
- Carbohydrates 53 g
- Sugar 45.5 g
- Protein 9.5 g
- Cholesterol 64 mg

Ingredients:
- 2 tbsp dulce de leche
- ½ cup milk
- 1 ½ cups vanilla ice cream

Directions:

- Add all ingredients into the creami pint. Refer to the quick start guide for bowl assembly.
- Press milkshake mode.
- Once processing is done, remove the milkshake and serve.

Cream Cheese Milkshake

Preparation Time: 5 minutes   Cooking Time: 5 minutes   Serve: 1

Nutritional Value (Amount Per Serving)
- Calories 297
- Fat 24.5 g
- Carbohydrates 12.5 g
- Sugar 9.9 g
- Protein 7.4 g
- Cholesterol 82 mg

Ingredients:
- ¼ cup milk
- ½ cup vanilla ice cream
- 2 oz cream cheese, softened

Directions:

- Add all ingredients into the creami pint. Refer to the quick start guide for bowl assembly.
- Press milkshake mode.
- Once processing is done, remove the milkshake and serve.

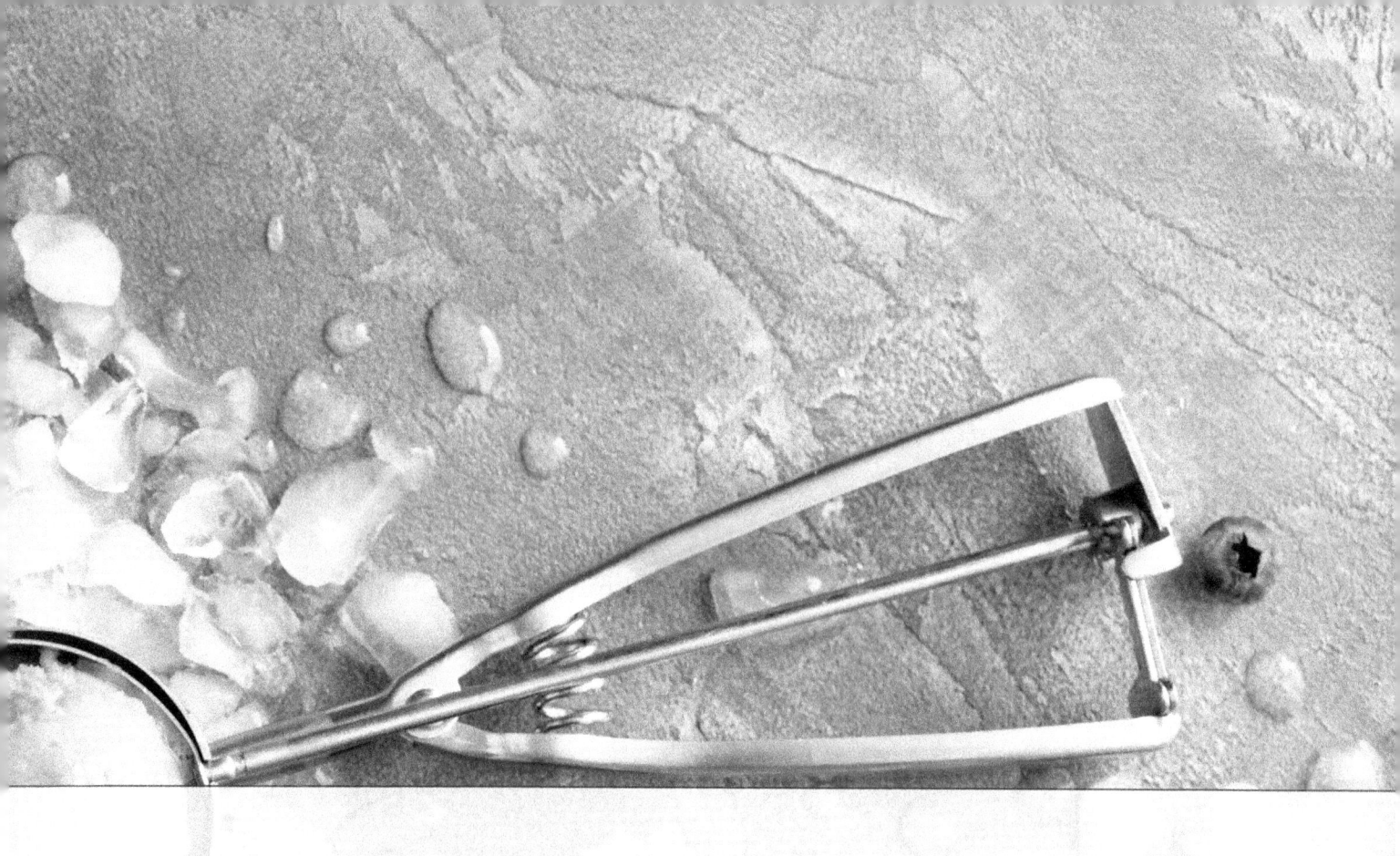

SORBET

Lemon Blueberry Sorbet

Preparation Time: 5 minutes   Cooking Time: 5 minutes   Serve: 2

Nutritional Value (Amount Per Serving)
- Calories 121
- Fat 2.5 g
- Carbohydrates 24.5 g
- Sugar 22.3 g
- Protein 1.7 g
- Cholesterol 8 mg

Ingredients:
- 1/3 cup blueberries
- 1 ½ cups lemonade
- ¼ cup milk
- 1 tbsp cream cheese, softened

Directions:

- In a bowl, mix together milk and cream cheese. Add blueberries and lemonade and mix well.
- Pour the sorbet mixture into the creami pint and cover the pint with a lid and place in the freezer for 24 hours.
- Remove pint from the freezer and take off the lid. Refer to the quick start guide for bowl assembly.
- Press sorbet mode.
- Once processing is done, remove sorbet and serve.

Mango Sorbet

Preparation Time: 5 minutes   Cooking Time: 5 minutes   Serve: 2

Nutritional Value (Amount Per Serving)
- Calories 126
- Fat 0 g
- Carbohydrates 9.5 g
- Sugar 26.8 g
- Protein 0 g
- Cholesterol 0 mg

Ingredients:
- 14 oz can mango

Directions:

- Add can mango with liquid into the creami pint and cover pint with lid and place in freezer for 24 hours.
- Remove pint from the freezer and take off the lid. Refer to the quick start guide for bowl assembly.
- Press sorbet mode.
- Once processing is done, remove sorbet and serve.

Orange Sorbet

Preparation Time: 5 minutes   Cooking Time: 5 minutes   Serve: 4

Nutritional Value (Amount Per Serving)
- Calories 86
- Fat 0.1 g
- Carbohydrates 23 g
- Sugar 22 g
- Protein 0.6 g
- Cholesterol 0 mg

Ingredients:
- 20 oz can mandarin oranges

Directions:

- Add can oranges with liquid into the creami pint and cover pint with lid and place in freezer for 24 hours.
- Remove pint from the freezer and take off the lid. Refer to the quick start guide for bowl assembly.
- Press sorbet mode.
- Once processing is done, remove sorbet and serve.

Peach Sorbet

Preparation Time: 5 minutes   Cooking Time: 5 minutes   Serve: 2

Nutritional Value (Amount Per Serving)
- Calories 107
- Fat 0.1 g
- Carbohydrates 28.9 g
- Sugar 26.3 g
- Protein 0.9 g
- Cholesterol 0 mg

Ingredients:
- 14 oz can peaches

Directions:

- Add can peaches with liquid into the creami pint and cover pint with lid and place in freezer for 24 hours.
- Remove pint from the freezer and take off the lid. Refer to the quick start guide for bowl assembly.
- Press sorbet mode.
- Once processing is done, remove sorbet and serve.

Pineapple Sorbet

Preparation Time: 5 minutes   Cooking Time: 5 minutes   Serve: 2

Nutritional Value (Amount Per Serving)
- Calories 136
- Fat 0.2 g
- Carbohydrates 35.6 g
- Sugar 32.8 g
- Protein 1 g
- Cholesterol 0 mg

Ingredients:
- 16 oz can pineapple

Directions:
- Add can pineapple with water into the creami pint and cover the pint with lid and place in freezer for 24 hours.
- Remove pint from the freezer and take off the lid. Refer to the quick start guide for bowl assembly.
- Press sorbet mode.
- Once processing is done, remove sorbet and serve.

Blueberry Sorbet

Preparation Time: 5 minutes   Cooking Time: 5 minutes   Serve: 4

Nutritional Value (Amount Per Serving)
- Calories 94
- Fat 0.4 g
- Carbohydrates 23.5 g
- Sugar 21.8 g
- Protein 0.7 g
- Cholesterol 0 mg

Ingredients:
- 15 oz can blueberries
- ½ cup water

Directions:

- Add can blueberry with their liquid and water into the creami pint and cover pint with lid and place in freezer for 24 hours.
- Remove pint from the freezer and take off the lid. Refer to the quick start guide for bowl assembly.
- Press sorbet mode.
- Once processing is done, remove sorbet and serve.

Lemon Sorbet

Preparation Time: 5 minutes   Cooking Time: 5 minutes   Serve: 4

Nutritional Value (Amount Per Serving)
- Calories 114
- Fat 0.2 g
- Carbohydrates 29.3 g
- Sugar 26.9 g
- Protein 0.2 g
- Cholesterol 0 mg

Ingredients:
- ½ cup fresh lemon juice
- 1 cup water
- 1 tbsp corn syrup
- ½ cup sugar

Directions:
- In a bowl, stir together water, corn syrup, sugar, and lemon juice until sugar is dissolved.
- Pour the sorbet mixture into the creami pint and cover the pint with a lid and place in the freezer for 24 hours.
- Remove pint from the freezer and take off the lid. Refer to the quick start guide for bowl assembly.
- Press sorbet mode.
- Once processing is done, remove sorbet and serve.

Raspberry Sorbet

Preparation Time: 5 minutes   Cooking Time: 5 minutes   Serve: 4

Nutritional Value (Amount Per Serving)
- Calories 277
- Fat 0.6 g
- Carbohydrates 72 g
- Sugar 58.1 g
- Protein 0.9 g
- Cholesterol 0 mg

Ingredients:
- 8 oz raspberries
- ¼ cup corn syrup
- 1 cup water
- 1 cup sugar
- 6 tbsp lemon juice

Directions:

- In a bowl, stir together water, sugar, lemon juice, and corn syrup until sugar is dissolved. Add raspberries and stir well.
- Pour the sorbet mixture into the creami pint and cover the pint with a lid and place in the freezer for 24 hours.
- Remove pint from the freezer and take off the lid. Refer to the quick start guide for bowl assembly.
- Press sorbet mode.
- Once processing is done, remove sorbet and serve.

Strawberry Balsamic Sorbet

Preparation Time: 5 minutes   Cooking Time: 5 minutes   Serve: 2

Nutritional Value (Amount Per Serving)
- Calories 151
- Fat 0.5 g
- Carbohydrates 38.5 g
- Sugar 33.7 g
- Protein 1.2 g
- Cholesterol 0 mg

Ingredients:
- 1 lb strawberries
- ½ tsp balsamic vinegar
- 6 tbsp sugar
- 1/3 cup orange juice

Directions:
- In a bowl, stir together orange juice and sugar until sugar is dissolved. Add balsamic vinegar and strawberries and stir well.
- Add sorbet mixture into the creami pint and cover pint with lid and place in freezer for 24 hours.
- Remove pint from the freezer and take off the lid. Refer to the quick start guide for bowl assembly.
- Press sorbet mode.
- Once processing is done, remove sorbet and serve.

Orange Basil Sorbet

Preparation Time: 5 minutes   Cooking Time: 5 minutes   Serve: 4

Nutritional Value (Amount Per Serving)
- Calories 199
- Fat 0.3 g
- Carbohydrates 50.7 g
- Sugar 47.9 g
- Protein 1.1 g
- Cholesterol 0 mg

Ingredients:
- 1 cup fresh basil
- 2 cups orange juice
- 1 tsp orange peel, shredded
- ¾ cup water
- ¾ cup sugar

Directions:
- In a bowl, stir together orange juice, water, and sugar until sugar is dissolved. Add orange peel and basil and stir well.
- Pour the sorbet mixture into the creami pint and cover the pint with a lid and place in the freezer for 24 hours.
- Remove pint from the freezer and take off the lid. Refer to the quick start guide for bowl assembly.
- Press sorbet mode.
- Once processing is done, remove sorbet and serve.

SMOOTHIE BOWL

Strawberry Smoothie

Preparation Time: 5 minutes   Cooking Time: 5 minutes   Serve: 4

Nutritional Value (Amount Per Serving)
- Calories 111
- Fat 2.2 g
- Carbohydrates 21.1 g
- Sugar 15.6 g
- Protein 3.8 g
- Cholesterol 8 mg

Ingredients:
- 2 cups strawberries
- 1 tbsp honey
- 1 banana, sliced
- 1 ½ cups milk

Directions:
- Add all ingredients into the creami pint and cover pint with lid and place in freezer for 24 hours.
- Remove pint from the freezer and take off the lid. Refer to the quick start guide for bowl assembly.
- Press smoothie bowl mode.
- Once processing is done, transfer the smoothie to a bowl and serve.

Banana Smoothie

Preparation Time: 5 minutes   Cooking Time: 5 minutes   Serve: 2

Nutritional Value (Amount Per Serving)
- Calories 309
- Fat 18 g
- Carbohydrates 35.7 g
- Sugar 15.3 g
- Protein 7.8 g
- Cholesterol 0 mg

Ingredients:
- 2 ripe bananas
- 1.5 oz ground almonds
- 4 cups unsweetened almond milk
- ¼ tsp cinnamon

Directions:
- Add all ingredients into the creami pint and cover pint with lid and place in freezer for 24 hours.
- Remove pint from the freezer and take off the lid. Refer to the quick start guide for bowl assembly.
- Press smoothie bowl mode.
- Once processing is done, transfer the smoothie to a bowl and serve.

Orange Mango Smoothie

Preparation Time: 5 minutes   Cooking Time: 5 minutes   Serve: 4

Nutritional Value (Amount Per Serving)
- Calories 277
- Fat 7.3 g
- Carbohydrates 50.3 g
- Sugar 31.6 g
- Protein 5.8 g
- Cholesterol 10 mg

Ingredients:
- 2 cups frozen mango
- 2 tsp chia seeds
- 2 cups orange juice
- 2 ripe bananas, sliced

Directions:
- Add all ingredients into the creami pint and cover pint with lid and place in freezer for 24 hours.
- Remove pint from the freezer and take off the lid. Refer to the quick start guide for bowl assembly.
- Press smoothie bowl mode.
- Once processing is done, transfer the smoothie to a bowl and serve.

Mixed Berry Smoothie

Preparation Time: 5 minutes   Cooking Time: 5 minutes   Serve: 4

Nutritional Value (Amount Per Serving)
- Calories 208
- Fat 7.2 g
- Carbohydrates 32.3 g
- Sugar 15.5 g
- Protein 4.4 g
- Cholesterol 0 mg

Ingredients:
- 16 oz frozen mixed berries
- ¼ cup flax seed meal
- 2 cups spinach
- 5 cups unsweetened almond milk
- 2 bananas, sliced

Directions:
- Add all ingredients into the creami pint and cover pint with lid and place in freezer for 24 hours.
- Remove pint from the freezer and take off the lid. Refer to the quick start guide for bowl assembly.
- Press smoothie bowl mode.
- Once processing is done, transfer the smoothie to a bowl and serve.

Raspberry Peach Smoothie

Preparation Time: 5 minutes   Cooking Time: 5 minutes   Serve: 2

Nutritional Value (Amount Per Serving)
- Calories 538
- Fat 34.8 g
- Carbohydrates 56.5 g
- Sugar 42.2 g
- Protein 8 g
- Cholesterol 0 mg

Ingredients:
- 2 cups water
- 1 cup coconut milk
- 2 tsp hemp seeds
- 1 tbsp chia seeds
- 1 lemon juice
- 1 cup frozen raspberries
- 1 ½ cups frozen peaches

Directions:

- Add all ingredients into the creami pint and cover pint with lid and place in freezer for 24 hours.
- Remove pint from the freezer and take off the lid. Refer to the quick start guide for bowl assembly.
- Press smoothie bowl mode.
- Once processing is done, transfer the smoothie to a bowl and serve.

Mango Raspberry Smoothie

Preparation Time: 5 minutes   Cooking Time: 5 minutes   Serve: 2

Nutritional Value (Amount Per Serving)
- Calories 274
- Fat 2.1 g
- Carbohydrates 67.4 g
- Sugar 51.7 g
- Protein 4.5 g
- Cholesterol 0 mg

Ingredients:
- 1 lime juice
- 15 mint leaves
- 2 mangoes, peel & dice
- 2 cups water
- 2 cups raspberries

Directions:
- Add all ingredients into the creami pint and cover pint with lid and place in freezer for 24 hours.
- Remove pint from the freezer and take off the lid. Refer to the quick start guide for bowl assembly.
- Press smoothie bowl mode.
- Once processing is done, transfer the smoothie to a bowl and serve.

Pina Colada Smoothie

Preparation Time: 5 minutes   Cooking Time: 5 minutes   Serve: 2

Nutritional Value (Amount Per Serving)
- Calories 626
- Fat 14.7 g
- Carbohydrates 113.5 g
- Sugar 95.4 g
- Protein 13.5 g
- Cholesterol 10 mg

Ingredients:
- 2 tbsp honey
- 2 cups coconut milk
- 12 oz vanilla yogurt
- 2 bananas, sliced
- 2 cups frozen pineapple chunks

Directions:

- Add all ingredients into the creami pint and cover pint with lid and place in freezer for 24 hours.
- Remove pint from the freezer and take off the lid. Refer to the quick start guide for bowl assembly.
- Press smoothie bowl mode.
- Once processing is done, transfer the smoothie to a bowl and serve.

Pumpkin Smoothie

Preparation Time: 5 minutes   Cooking Time: 5 minutes   Serve: 2

Nutritional Value (Amount Per Serving)
- Calories 187
- Fat 3.3 g
- Carbohydrates 29.8 g
- Sugar 23 g
- Protein 9.2 g
- Cholesterol 13 mg

Ingredients:
- 1 cup pumpkin puree
- 1/8 tsp cinnamon
- ½ tsp pumpkin pie spice
- 2 tbsp brown sugar
- 6 oz vanilla yogurt
- ½ tsp vanilla extract
- ¾ cup milk

Directions:
- Add all ingredients into the creami pint and cover pint with lid and place in freezer for 24 hours.
- Remove pint from the freezer and take off the lid. Refer to the quick start guide for bowl assembly.
- Press smoothie bowl mode.
- Once processing is done, transfer the smoothie to a bowl and serve.

Pineapple Strawberry Smoothie

Preparation Time: 5 minutes   Cooking Time: 5 minutes   Serve: 2

Nutritional Value (Amount Per Serving)
- Calories 389
- Fat 27.7 g
- Carbohydrates 39 g
- Sugar 27.1 g
- Protein 4.5 g
- Cholesterol 0 mg

Ingredients:
- 2 cups pineapple chunks
- 2 cups strawberries
- 8 oz almond milk

Directions:
- Add all ingredients into the creami pint and cover pint with lid and place in freezer for 24 hours.
- Remove pint from the freezer and take off the lid. Refer to the quick start guide for bowl assembly.
- Press smoothie bowl mode.
- Once processing is done, transfer the smoothie to a bowl and serve.

Mango Banana Pineapple Smoothie

Preparation Time: 5 minutes   Cooking Time: 5 minutes   Serve: 3

Nutritional Value (Amount Per Serving)
- Calories 209
- Fat 3 g
- Carbohydrates 40.6 g
- Sugar 30.4 g
- Protein 7.7 g
- Cholesterol 9 mg

Ingredients:
- ¾ cup orange juice
- ¾ cup Greek yogurt
- ½ cup banana
- 1 cup frozen mango
- 2 cups pineapple chunks

Directions:
- Add all ingredients into the creami pint and cover pint with lid and place in freezer for 24 hours.
- Remove pint from the freezer and take off the lid. Refer to the quick start guide for bowl assembly.
- Press smoothie bowl mode.
- Once processing is done, transfer the smoothie to a bowl and serve.

Banana Peanut Butter Smoothie

Preparation Time: 5 minutes   Cooking Time: 5 minutes   Serve: 2

Nutritional Value (Amount Per Serving)
- Calories 351
- Fat 21.4 g
- Carbohydrates 27.3 g
- Sugar 12.6 g
- Protein 17 g
- Cholesterol 8 mg

Ingredients:
- 2 cups unsweetened almond milk
- ¼ cup peanut butter
- ¼ cup rolled oats
- ½ cup Greek yogurt
- 2 frozen bananas

Directions:
- Add all ingredients into the creami pint and cover pint with lid and place in freezer for 24 hours.
- Remove pint from the freezer and take off the lid. Refer to the quick start guide for bowl assembly.
- Press smoothie bowl mode.
- Once processing is done, transfer the smoothie to a bowl and serve.

Coffee Banana Smoothie

Preparation Time: 5 minutes   Cooking Time: 5 minutes   Serve: 2

Nutritional Value (Amount Per Serving)
- Calories 179
- Fat 3.3 g
- Carbohydrates 34.7 g
- Sugar 20.3 g
- Protein 5.9 g
- Cholesterol 10 mg

Ingredients:
- 1 cup brewed coffee
- 1 cup milk
- 1 tbsp cocoa powder
- 2 bananas
- 1 tsp vanilla

Directions:
- Add all ingredients into the creami pint and cover pint with lid and place in freezer for 24 hours.
- Remove pint from the freezer and take off the lid. Refer to the quick start guide for bowl assembly.
- Press smoothie bowl mode.
- Once processing is done, transfer the smoothie to a bowl and serve.

Blueberry Oat Smoothie

Preparation Time: 5 minutes   Cooking Time: 5 minutes   Serve: 2

Nutritional Value (Amount Per Serving)
- Calories 340
- Fat 9.5 g
- Carbohydrates 55.8 g
- Sugar 26.9 g
- Protein 12.3 g
- Cholesterol 13 mg

Ingredients:
- 1 banana
- 1 tbsp chia seeds
- 1 cup milk
- 5 oz blueberry yogurt
- 1 cup spinach
- ½ cup old-fashioned oats
- 1/3 cup blueberries

Directions:

- Add all ingredients into the creami pint and cover pint with lid and place in freezer for 24 hours.
- Remove pint from the freezer and take off the lid. Refer to the quick start guide for bowl assembly.
- Press smoothie bowl mode.
- Once processing is done, transfer the smoothie to a bowl and serve.

Tropical Smoothie

Preparation Time: 5 minutes   Cooking Time: 5 minutes   Serve: 2

Nutritional Value (Amount Per Serving)
- Calories 292
- Fat 3.5 g
- Carbohydrates 64.7 g
- Sugar 42.8 g
- Protein 5.5 g
- Cholesterol 10 mg

Ingredients:
- 2 bananas
- 2 cups coconut water
- 1 cup pineapple
- 1 cup frozen mango

Directions:

- Add all ingredients into the creami pint and cover pint with lid and place in freezer for 24 hours.
- Remove pint from the freezer and take off the lid. Refer to the quick start guide for bowl assembly.
- Press smoothie bowl mode.
- Once processing is done, transfer the smoothie to a bowl and serve.

Orange Smoothie

Preparation Time: 5 minutes   Cooking Time: 5 minutes   Serve: 4

Nutritional Value (Amount Per Serving)
- Calories 119
- Fat 0.4 g
- Carbohydrates 28.9 g
- Sugar 22.8 g
- Protein 1.2 g
- Cholesterol 0 mg

Ingredients:
- 2 cups orange juice
- 1 tsp cinnamon
- 1 tsp vanilla
- 2 tbsp honey
- 1 banana

Directions:

- Add all ingredients into the creami pint and cover pint with lid and place in freezer for 24 hours.
- Remove pint from the freezer and take off the lid. Refer to the quick start guide for bowl assembly.
- Press smoothie bowl mode.
- Once processing is done, transfer the smoothie to a bowl and serve.

CONCLUSION

The Ninja CREAMi treat maker is one of the revolutionary advanced ice cream maker machines used to make flavourful ice cream treats at home. It comes with a dual motor base and takes 800Watts power to churn your favourite frozen treat into the cream. It also allows you to add your favourite Mix-in into your favourite ice cream. It is one of the multifunctional kitchen appliances not only make ice cream but is also used to make your favorite milkshake, smoothies, sorbet, gelato, and more.

This cookbook contains 80 delicious and healthy Ninja CREAMi treat recipes. All the recipes written in this cookbook are unique and written in an easy to understandable format. The recipes written in this cookbook are beginning with their exact preparation and processing time followed by a set of step-by-step process instructions. All the recipe ends with its nutritional value information. The nutritional value information will help to keep track of daily calorie consumption.

happy cooking

APPENDIX RECIPE INDEX

A
Avocado Ice Cream 034
Almond milk Ice Cream 035
Almond Coconut Ice Cream 051

B
Banana Milkshake 057
Berry Cheesecake Milkshake 064
Blackberry Milkshake 065
Blueberry Milkshake 066
Blueberry Sorbet 080
Banana Smoothie 087
Banana Peanut Butter Smoothie 096
Blueberry Oat Smoothie 098

C
Chocolate Ice Cream 019
Cream Cheese Ice Cream 022
Coconut Ice Cream 023
Chocolate Peanut Butter Ice Cream 031
Coffee Ice Cream 033
Coconut Maple Ice Cream 037
Cookie Ice Cream 038
Chocolate Almond Ice Cream..... 039
Choco Chip Orange Ice Cream ...040
Chocolate Chip Ice Cream 041
Choco Chip Cookie Dough Ice Cream 043
Coffee Choco Chip Ice Cream 045
Chocolate Toffee Crunch Ice Cream 048
Chocolate Cashew Ice Cream 049
Chocolate Caramel Ice Cream 050
Chocolate Cookie Ice Cream 052
Coffee Milkshake 056
Chocolate Banana Milkshake 058
Chocolate Milkshake 060
Choco Banana Peanut Butter Milkshake 063
Coconut Mango Milkshake 068
Chocolate Protein Shake.............070
Caramel Milkshake....................... 071
Cream Cheese Milkshake 073
Coffee Banana Smoothie 097

D
Death by Chocolate Ice Cream ... 042
Dulce de Leche Milkshake........... 072

K
Key Lime Pie Ice Cream............... 025

L
Lemon Ice Cream 036
Lemon Blueberry Sorbet 075
Lemon Sorbet................................ 081

M
Maple Ice Cream 024
Mango Ice Cream 029
Maple Walnut Ice Cream 044
Mango Milkshake 069
Mango Sorbet 076
Mixed Berry Smoothie 089
Mango Raspberry Smoothie........091
Mango Banana Pineapple Smoothie 095

N
Nutella Milkshake........................ 054

O
Orange Ice Cream........................020
Orange Sorbet 077
Orange Basil Sorbet.................... 084
Orange Mango Smoothie 088
Orange Smoothie......................... 100

P
Pumpkin Pie Ice Cream 026
Pineapple Coconut Ice Cream 027
Pumpkin Ice Cream 028
Peanut Butter Ice Cream 030
Peach Ice Cream 032
Pistachio Ice Cream..................... 046
Peanut Butter Milkshake............. 061
Pumpkin Pie Milkshake 062
Peach Sorbet................................ 078
Pineapple Sorbet......................... 079
Raisin Rum Ice Cream 047
Raspberry Sorbet........................ 082
Raspberry Peach Smoothie........ 090

S
Strawberry Ice Cream 021
Strawberry Milkshake.................. 055
Strawberry Balsamic Sorbet 083
Strawberry Smoothie 086

T
Tropical Smoothie 099

V
Vanilla Ice Cream......................... 018
Vanilla Milkshake 059

W
White Chocolate Milkshake 067